Grand Times

special memories with your grandkids

Grand Times

This journal is part of The Gifts of being Grand
product collection, inspired by the well-loved gift book,
The Gifts of being Grand, a tribute to the special
joys and rewards of grandparenthood,
written and illustrated by Marianne Richmond.

©2004 by Marianne Richmond Studios, Inc.
All rights reserved. No part of this book
may be reproduced in any form without
written permission from the publisher.

Marianne Richmond Studios, Inc.
420 N. 5th Street, Suite 840
Minneapolis, MN 55401
www.mariannerichmond.com

ISBN 0-9741465-0-1

Text and illustrations by Marianne Richmond

Book design by Meg Anderson

Printed in China

First Printing

About this Journal

We created **Grand Times** because we know how special and memorable the gifts of grandparenthood can be! This keepsake journal is interactive – a book that inspires grandchild involvement as well as lets you create a one-of-a-kind treasured momento.

This journal features four sections:

Grand Days Remembered – Record here highlights of your special times together. Record the date, a synopsis of the day's events and the little things that made you and your grandkid(s) laugh.

Spoken Treasures – Kids really do say laugh-out-loud things. Record here cute comments, funny questions, or the humorous stories that you know you'll share with an appreciative ear. We've featured here some clever quips to make you smile.

Grand-o-Grams – Any season is a reason to be in touch with your grandchildren! Use these 20 fun postcards to say hello, send a hug, or to remind them how much you love them. You may even inspire a return letter!

Grand Momentos – Use this section to create your own scrapbook of memories. Paste favorite pictures. Save ticket stubs or meaningful notes and cards. Save those precious pieces of artwork. Or trace the 3-year-old hand that grows so quickly.

date _____

What we did today

_____
_____
_____
_____
_____
_____
_____

My / our favorite part of the day

_____
_____
_____
_____
_____
_____

My / our favorite part of the day

_____

_____

_____

_____

_____

_____

What made me / us laugh

_____

_____

_____

_____

_____

_____

date _____

What we did today

_____
_____
_____
_____
_____
_____

My / our favorite part of the day

_____
_____
_____
_____
_____
_____

My / our favorite part of the day

_____

_____

_____

_____

_____

_____

What made me / us laugh

_____

_____

_____

_____

_____

_____

_____

date _____

What we did today

_____

_____

_____

_____

_____

_____

_____

My / our favorite part of the day

_____

_____

_____

_____

_____

_____

My / our favorite part of the day

_____

_____

_____

_____

_____

_____

What made me / us laugh

_____

_____

_____

_____

_____

_____

date _____

What we did today

_____
_____
_____
_____
_____
_____
_____

My / our favorite part of the day

_____
_____
_____
_____
_____
_____

My / our favorite part of the day

_____

_____

_____

_____

_____

_____

What made me / us laugh

_____

_____

_____

_____

_____

_____

_____

date _____

What we did today

_____
_____
_____
_____
_____
_____
_____

My / our favorite part of the day

_____
_____
_____
_____
_____
_____

My / our favorite part of the day

_____

_____

_____

_____

_____

_____

What made me / us laugh

_____

_____

_____

_____

_____

_____

_____

date _____

What we did today

_____
_____
_____
_____
_____
_____
_____

My / our favorite part of the day

_____
_____
_____
_____
_____
_____

My / our favorite part of the day

_____

_____

_____

_____

_____

_____

What made me / us laugh

_____

_____

_____

_____

_____

_____

date _____

What we did today

_____
_____
_____
_____
_____
_____
_____

My / our favorite part of the day

_____
_____
_____
_____
_____
_____
_____

My / our favorite part of the day

_____

_____

_____

_____

_____

_____

What made me / us laugh

_____

_____

_____

_____

_____

_____

date _____

What we did today

_____
_____
_____
_____
_____
_____

My / our favorite part of the day

_____
_____
_____
_____
_____
_____

My / our favorite part of the day

_____

_____

_____

_____

_____

_____

_____

What made me / us laugh

_____

_____

_____

_____

_____

_____

_____

_____

A grandmother was telling her little granddaughter what her own childhood was like: "We used to skate outside on a pond. I had a swing made from a tire, it hung from a tree in our front yard. We rode our pony. We picked wild raspberries in the woods."

The little girl was wide-eyed, taking this in. At last she said, "I sure wish I'd gotten to know you sooner!"

A sweet little boy surprised his grandmother one morning and brought her a cup of coffee. He made it himself and was so proud. He anxiously waited to hear the verdict on the quality of the coffee. The grandmother had never in her life had such a bad cup of coffee, and as she forced down the last sip, she noticed three of those little green army guys in the bottom of the cup.

She asked, "Honey, why would three little green army guys be in the bottom of my cup?"

Her grandson replied, "You know grandma, it's like on TV, 'The best part of waking up is soldiers in your cup.'"

I didn't know if my granddaughter had learned her colors yet, so I decided to test her. I would point out something and ask her what color it was. She would tell me, and she always was correct. But it was fun for me, so I continued. At last she headed for the door, saying sagely, "Grandma, I think you should try to figure out some of these yourself."

"Dear God, please take care of my daddy, mommy, sister, brother, my doggy and me. Oh, please take care of yourself, God. If anything happens to you, we're gonna be in a big mess."

Grand Momentos

Use this section to create your own scrapbook of memories. Paste favorite pictures. Save ticket stubs or meaningful notes and cards. Save those precious pieces of artwork. Or trace the 3-year-old hand that grows so quickly.